CHRISTY MOORE

27 Career Transition Tips

Use the Job You Have to Get the Job You Want

First edition

This book was professionally typeset on Reedsy.
Find out more at reedsy.com

Contents

1

Introduction

Imagine you're standing at a crossroads in your career. One path is the comfortable, well-trodden road you've been on for years. The other? A new, uncharted path towards the career you've always wanted. This book is your guide to making that crucial leap from the job you have to the job you want.

I'm not just a bystander in this journey. Like you, I've faced the uncertainty and excitement of a career transition. Drawing from my own experiences, I've crafted this book to be your career transition toolkit. It's packed with 27 simple yet powerful tips that you can apply right now, regardless of where you are in your professional journey.

Here's the thing about career transitions: they're not just about changing jobs. They're about transforming your outlook, leveraging your current position, and strategically positioning yourself for new opportunities. Whether it's mastering the art of networking, crafting a resume that stands out, or navigating the nuances of your current work environment, each tip is a stepping stone towards your dream job.

The book is divided into three essential areas: Work Environment, Resume & Interviewing, and Networking. In the Work Environment section, you'll learn how to maximize your current role as a launchpad for your next big move. It's about more than just doing your job; it's about learning, growing, and positioning yourself as an invaluable asset.

Next, in Resume & Interviewing, we dive into the art of self-presentation. It's not just about listing your experiences; it's about telling your story in a way that resonates with your future employers. You'll learn how to tailor your resume for a new career and ace interviews with confidence and authenticity.

Finally, in Networking, you'll discover the power of connections. Networking isn't just about collecting contacts; it's about building meaningful relationships that open doors to opportunities you never knew existed. This section will equip you with practical strategies to expand your professional network in ways that feel authentic and empowering.

By the end of this book, you'll have a clear road map for using your current job as a springboard to the career you've always desired. You'll be equipped with practical, actionable tips to make your transition smoother and more successful.

So, let's embark on this journey together. Turn the page, and let's start transforming your career, one tip at a time.

2

The Work Environment

This chapter focuses on recognizing potential pathways to a new role within your existing work environment. It explores strategies for identifying individuals and opportunities that can serve as stepping stones for career advancement. By examining your current surroundings and connections, you can uncover valuable avenues for making a successful transition to a new role.

Identify Internal Influencers

To navigate your career path successfully within your current organization, identifying internal influencers is crucial. These are individuals who, regardless of their official titles, wield significant influence through their expertise, connections, and respect they command. Start by observing who colleagues often turn to for advice, who leads discussions in meetings, and whose opinions seem to sway decisions. These influencers often mentor others and are central in networks, making them key allies in your career journey.

Engaging with them involves more than casual interactions; it's about building genuine relationships based on shared interests and mutual respect. By aligning yourself with these influencers and learning from their insights, you open doors to mentorship, wider networks, and a deeper understanding of the organizational dynamics. Their endorsement can be invaluable as you seek new opportunities within the company, making them integral to your strategy for career advancement.

Join a Business Resource Group (BRG)

Business Resource Groups (BRGs), also referred to as Employee Resource Groups, are invaluable platforms within organizations that promote inclusivity and foster professional development. These groups are typically centered around shared characteristics or interests, such as ethnicity, gender, or career interests, and provide a space for employees to connect, learn from one another, and support each other.

Joining a BRG is a strategic move for career advancement as it offers access to networking opportunities, mentorship, and professional workshops. Participation in these groups can increase your visibility within the organization, particularly with senior leadership often involved in these initiatives. BRGs also offer a unique perspective on the company's diversity and inclusion efforts, allowing you to contribute to meaningful projects and discussions.

Actively engaging in a BRG not only enriches your professional experience but also positions you as an involved and proactive member of your organizational community, enhancing your profile for future career opportunities.

Seek Mentorship

Mentoring is a pivotal element in career development, providing personalized guidance, knowledge sharing, and opportunities for professional growth. A mentorship relationship pairs you with someone more experienced in your field, providing a platform for you to gain insights, develop new skills, and navigate the complexities of your career path. Engaging in a mentor-mentee relationship enables the exchange of experiences, fostering both personal and professional growth.

A mentor can offer invaluable advice on career decisions, help you identify and achieve your career goals, and introduce you to broader networks. Seeking a mentor within your organization can also provide an insider's perspective on navigating workplace dynamics and identifying growth opportunities. Actively participating in mentorship demonstrates your commitment to learning and growth, a trait highly valued in professional settings.

By embracing mentoring, you not only enrich your career journey but also prepare yourself for future roles, including becoming a mentor to others, thereby perpetuating a culture of learning and development.

Apply for a Job Rotation

Job rotations in an organization offer a unique opportunity to experience different roles and departments. These rotations act as stepping stones, allowing you to broaden your skill set, understand various aspects of the business, and establish a diverse professional network. By working in multiple areas, you gain a holistic view of the organization, which is invaluable in understanding where your skills and interests best align.

This variety of experience makes you a more versatile and attractive candidate for future roles, both within and outside your current organization. Rotations also demonstrate your adaptability and willingness to learn, traits that are highly desirable in the dynamic modern workplace.

Engaging in job rotations positions you not just as an employee performing a specific function, but as a well-rounded professional with a comprehensive understanding of the business, paving the way for a successful career transition.

Volunteer

Volunteering, both within and outside your organization, allows you to showcase and enhance skills that may not be utilized in your current role, providing a broader platform to demonstrate your capabilities and potential. Intra-organizational volunteering, like participating in committees or corporate social responsibility initiatives, increases your visibility across different departments and introduces you to new networks, often including senior leadership.

Externally, volunteering in industry-related organizations or community projects can expand your professional network beyond your current company and expose you to new industry trends and opportunities. This involvement not only enriches your resume but also demonstrates your initiative, adaptability, and commitment to continuous learning and growth. Volunteering positions you as a well-rounded and socially conscious individual, making you an attractive candidate for potential employers and paving the way for a successful career move.

Connect with Vendors

Establishing connections with vendors and external partners who collaborate with your company can strategically offer a unique external perspective on your industry, providing insights into market trends, emerging technologies, and best practices. By interacting with vendors, you not only broaden your professional network beyond your immediate organization but also gain a deeper understanding of the broader industry landscape.

These relationships can reveal new opportunities, including potential job openings or collaborations that align with your career aspirations. Moreover, vendors can provide valuable endorsements or referrals, leveraging their industry-wide connections. Engaging with vendors demonstrates your proactive approach to understanding the full spectrum of your industry, highlighting your versatility and strategic thinking to potential employers.

This external networking is a key component in positioning yourself for a successful transition to new roles or career paths.

Make a Lateral Career Move

Making a lateral career move, where you shift to a different but equivalent role within your organization, can be a highly strategic decision for long-term career growth. This move allows you to diversify your skill set and gain experience in different areas of the business, making you a more well-rounded professional. It exposes you to new teams, projects, and challenges, broadening your internal network and understanding of the company.

A lateral move can also reinvigorate your career by offering a fresh perspective and new learning opportunities, keeping your work experience dynamic and engaging. Furthermore, it demonstrates your flexibility and adaptability to potential

employers, showcasing your ability to thrive in diverse environments. While it may not immediately lead to a higher position, a
lateral move strategically positions you for future upward career
advancements by equipping you with a more comprehensive set
of skills and experiences.

Participate in Projects for Career Advancement

Participation in diverse projects, especially those outside your
regular scope of work, allows you to showcase and enhance your
skills in a real-world context. It provides exposure to different
aspects of the business, broadening your understanding and
experience. This involvement also increases your visibility
within the company, especially with project leaders and team
members from different departments.

By actively contributing to projects, you demonstrate your
initiative, problem-solving abilities, and capacity to work collaboratively, traits valued in any professional setting. Additionally, successful project involvement can lead to significant
achievements and accomplishments that can be highlighted in
your resume and discussed in future job interviews. Thus, taking
part in projects is not just about the immediate outcomes but
about building a portfolio of experiences and skills that pave the
way for future career opportunities.

The Impact of Attire

Attire plays a subtle yet significant role in professional settings, influencing perceptions and potentially impacting career progression. Dressing appropriately for your workplace demonstrates respect for the organization and an understanding of its culture. It can also influence how you are perceived by colleagues and superiors, often contributing to first impressions.

Wearing attire that aligns with the expected standards of your role, or slightly above, can project professionalism, competence, and attention to detail. This is particularly important in client-facing roles or when representing your company in external meetings. Moreover, dressing well can boost your confidence, impacting your demeanor and performance.

While attire should not override merit and capability, it is an element of personal branding that can subtly influence your career trajectory, making it an aspect worth considering in your professional life.

3

Resumè & Interviewing

In this chapter, we dive into the art of crafting a resume tailored for the job you want and mastering interviews, especially when explaining your career transition. It's about strategically presenting your past experiences and skills in a way that aligns seamlessly with your future ambitions.

Conduct Industry and Company Research

Conducting thorough industry and company research equips you with a deeper understanding of the industry's current trends, challenges, and future outlook, allowing you to align your skills and experiences with what is most relevant and in demand. Understanding a company's culture, values, and business objectives enables you to tailor your application materials, like your resume and cover letter, to resonate more closely with the employer's needs.

In interviews, this knowledge demonstrates your genuine interest and proactive approach, showing that you are not only well-informed but also enthusiastic about contributing to the company's success. Additionally, researching the industry and specific companies can help you identify potential networking opportunities and informational interviews, further increasing your chances of a successful transition.

In essence, comprehensive research is a strategic tool that positions you as an informed and dedicated candidate, significantly enhancing your prospects in a new career field.

Showcase Transferable Skills

Transferable skills are skills that are valuable across various job roles and industries, such as communication, leadership, problem-solving, and adaptability. When transitioning to a new career, these skills bridge the gap between your past experiences and the requirements of your new role.

Highlighting transferable skills on your resume and during interviews demonstrates your capability to adapt and thrive in different environments. They provide a compelling argument for why you are suitable for the new role, even if you lack specific industry experience. Emphasizing these skills shows potential employers that you possess a versatile skill set that can contribute to various aspects of the job, making you a valuable and adaptable asset in the face of changing business needs.

In essence, transferable skills are the cornerstone of a successful career pivot, offering a solid foundation upon which to build new, role-specific expertise.

Leverage Courses and Certifications

Pursuing courses and obtaining specialized certifications can be a game-changer in career transitions, especially when moving into a new field or industry. They demonstrate your commitment to acquiring the necessary skills and knowledge for your desired role. Courses and certifications can fill gaps in your expertise, making you a more competitive candidate by aligning your skill set with the specific requirements of the new job.

They also signal to potential employers your dedication to continuous learning and staying updated with industry trends and technologies. Additionally, these educational pursuits can expand your professional network, connecting you with instructors, peers, and industry professionals who can provide support, advice, and potentially job leads.

Investing in relevant education and certifications is a strategic move that not only enhances your skills and knowledge but also significantly boosts your credibility and attractiveness to employers in a new career field.

Tailor Your Resume

To tailor your resume for your dream job, start by meticulously analyzing the job description. Identify key skills and experiences that the role demands, and then reflect these in your resume, emphasizing relevant transferable skills and accomplishments from your current and past positions.

This process involves more than listing your previous roles; it's about strategically marketing yourself for your future career. Focus on aligning your skills with those highlighted in the job description and use a clear, professional format for your resume to ensure hiring managers can easily see why you're the ideal candidate. Replace generic objectives with a tailored career summary at the top of your resume, summarizing your professional background and how it aligns with the job you're targeting.

Here's an example of a summary for someone who want to transition from customer service to sales:

"*Results-oriented customer service professional with a strong track record of delivering exceptional customer experiences and exceeding performance targets. Seeking to leverage my exceptional communication and problem-solving skills to transition into a dynamic sales role, where I can drive revenue growth, build lasting client relationships, and contribute to the success of a high-performing sales team.*"

By mirroring the language of the job description and keeping your content updated and relevant, you transform your resume from a simple career overview into a compelling narrative that showcases your readiness for this new opportunity.

Tailor Your Cover Letter

A tailored cover letter can significantly enhance your job application. It's your opportunity to directly address the employer and explain why you're a perfect fit for the position, going beyond the resume to tell your story. A well-crafted cover letter allows you to draw connections between your past experiences and the job requirements, highlighting transferable skills and explaining how your unique background makes you an ideal candidate.

It's also a chance to showcase your knowledge about the company and express genuine enthusiasm for the role, demonstrating that you've done your homework and are seriously invested in the opportunity. Personalizing each cover letter to the specific job and employer shows that you're not just casting a wide net, but are thoughtfully applying to roles that align with your career goals. In essence, a tailored cover letter can make your application stand out, providing context and personality to your professional qualifications.

Tips for Effective Interviewing Practice

Practicing interviews, especially if it has been a while since your last interview, can significantly enhance your performance and boost your confidence. Here are some valuable tips:

1. Self-Assessment: Start by self-assessing your skills, experiences, and career goals. Identify areas that might require additional attention or explanation, particularly those related to your career gap.

2. Research Common Questions: Familiarize yourself with common interview questions relevant to your field and role. This ensures you're prepared to discuss your qualifications and address any gaps in your career history.

3. Use the STAR Method: Structure your responses using the STAR method (Situation, Task, Action, Result) to provide clear and concise answers. This format helps you articulate your experiences effectively.

4. Mock Interviews: Conduct mock interviews with a friend, family member, or professional coach. They can simulate real interview scenarios, offer constructive feedback, and help you refine your responses.

5. Record and Review: Record your mock interviews and review them to assess your body language, tone, and overall presentation. This helps you identify areas for improvement.

6. Stay Updated: Stay informed about industry trends and developments. This knowledge demonstrates your commitment to staying relevant.

7. Build Confidence: Practice not only your responses but also your overall interview demeanor. Confidence is key to making a positive impression.

8. Tailor Your Answers: Customize your responses to the specific job and company you're interviewing with. Show that you've done your homework and are genuinely interested.

9. Ask for Feedback: After mock interviews, seek feedback on your performance and areas that need enhancement. Use this input to refine your approach.

10. Stay Positive: Embrace the process as a learning opportunity. A positive attitude will help you overcome any interview jitters and present your best self.

By following these tips and dedicating time to interview practice, you can refine your interviewing skills, address any concerns about career gaps, and boost your confidence in the job market, ultimately improving your chances of a successful career transition.

Master Answering Interview Questions Using the STAR Method

Effectively answering interview questions about your career transition can significantly impact your job prospects. Employers often seek to understand your reasons for the change and how your past experiences make you suitable for the new role. The STAR method (Situation, Task, Action, Result) is an excellent framework for structuring your responses.

This method enables you to concisely and coherently present real-life examples, demonstrating your skills and experiences in a manner relevant to the new position.

Example:

Question: "Can you describe a time when you successfully adapted to a significant change at work?"

STAR Answer:
   - *Situation*: "In my previous role as a marketing coordinator, our company decided to shift from traditional marketing to a digital-first strategy."

- *Task*: "I was tasked with leading the transition for my team, despite my limited experience in digital marketing."

- *Action*: "I proactively enrolled in an online digital marketing course and collaborated closely with our IT department to understand the tools and platforms we would be using. I also organized weekly training sessions for my team to ensure everyone was up to speed."

- *Result*: "Within three months, our team successfully transitioned to the new strategy. We increased our digital engagement by 40% and saw a 25% rise in online sales, demonstrating our ability to adapt and thrive in the new digital environment."

Using the STAR method to frame your responses not only provides clarity but also showcases your problem-solving skills, adaptability, and ability to drive results – qualities that are highly valued in any career transition.

Creation of a 30-60-90-Day Transition Plan

Creating a 30-60-90-day plan, or a detailed transition plan, outlines your objectives and strategies for the first three months in the new role, demonstrating your proactivity, foresight, and commitment to success. It helps you establish clear goals, identify key areas where you need to develop skills, and plan how to integrate effectively into the new team and company culture.

Presenting this plan during interviews shows potential employers that you are not only serious about the role but also prepared to hit the ground running. It also serves as a personal road map, guiding your focus and actions during the initial critical period of your new job.

19

A well-thought-out plan can ease the transition process, accelerate your learning curve, and quickly demonstrate your value to the new team, setting a strong foundation for future success in your new career.

Get Personal Recommendations

Securing personal recommendations is a valuable strategy for networking as well as providing endorsements of your skills. To begin, identify individuals who can provide meaningful endorsements, such as former supervisors, colleagues, mentors, or clients with whom you've closely collaborated. When reaching out to them, personalize your request by explaining your career transition and its significance, while also reminding them of specific projects or experiences you shared.

Offering guidance on the key skills and qualities you'd like them to highlight can help tailor their recommendations to your new career goals. Providing your updated resume is also beneficial for context. Once they agree, graciously follow up with a thank-you message, and after submission, express your gratitude again. Building reciprocal relationships and utilizing LinkedIn for recommendations can further enhance your professional network.

Staying in touch with your recommenders, even post-transition, fosters ongoing connections and potential future opportunities. These personalized endorsements strengthen your professional image and reinforce your qualifications, making your transition smoother and more successful.

4

Networking

In career transitions, it's as much about who you know as what you know. This chapter explores networking through everyday interactions, not just formal business events. Your jogging neighbor, fellow soccer parent, or book club members are part of a valuable network. They know you beyond your job title, understanding your character and goals. This forms a network based on real relationships, offering a wealth of untapped opportunities.

Network with Leadership

When networking with leaders, a strategic and respectful approach is key. Begin by researching their background and current projects to gain insight into their challenges and interests. Initiate contact, whether by email, LinkedIn, or in person, with an acknowledgment of their work or recent accomplishments, demonstrating genuine respect for their expertise.

Be clear and concise about your intentions, whether you're seeking advice, insights, or discussing opportunities, and ask targeted questions or propose ideas relevant to their field. Consider what you can offer in return, as leaders value reciprocal relationships. Finally, effective follow-up, such as a thank-you message or updates on how their advice has aided you, is crucial in fostering a lasting and positive professional relationship with these individuals.

This approach extends beyond immediate benefits, focusing on establishing long-term, sustainable connections with leaders.

Be Active in Associations

Utilizing associations for networking involves active participation and engagement. Attend events and workshops to meet like-minded professionals, and volunteer for roles within the association to showcase your skills and dedication. In these settings, contribute to discussions and show a genuine interest in others' views.

Additionally, utilize online resources, such as forums and member directories, to identify and connect with potential contacts. Approach them with personalized messages, leveraging your shared association membership to build a foundation of trust and common interest.

Master using LinkedIn

To leverage LinkedIn for a career transition, first refine your profile to mirror your new career aspirations, highlighting relevant skills and experiences. Actively network by connecting with industry professionals and recruiters, personalizing each request. Engage consistently by commenting on posts and participating in group discussions to increase your visibility.

Utilize LinkedIn's job search tools, setting alerts for roles in your target field and following potential employers. Additionally, establish your presence in the new industry by regularly publishing articles or posts related to your career interests, which helps build your professional brand and demonstrates your expertise in the new domain.

Consider subscribing to LinkedIn Premium to gain additional information and insights about job openings and companies.

Connect with Recruiters

To effectively use recruiters for a career transition, it's vital to select those with expertise in your target industry. Clearly communicate your career objectives, strengths, and the kind of role you're seeking. Be transparent about your experiences and aspirations. Regularly update them on any changes in your career goals or qualifications.

Recruiters can provide valuable insights on resume enhancement, interview techniques, and the current job market in your desired field. Engaging actively with the opportunities they suggest and responding promptly to their communications are key. Also, utilize their network for introductions to industry insiders and informational interviews, which can offer deeper insights and potentially uncover hidden job opportunities.

Building a strong, collaborative relationship with your recruiters can significantly aid in navigating your career transition effectively.

Conduct Informational Interviews

Using informational interviews for career transition is a strategic approach to gain industry insights and build your network. Begin by identifying professionals in your target field and reach out to them with a concise and respectful request for a brief informational interview.

Prepare specific questions about their career path, industry trends, and advice for someone transitioning into the field. During the interview, be an active listener and express genuine interest in their experiences. It's also an opportunity to briefly share your background and career aspirations, but keep the focus on learning from their journey.

Follow up with a thank-you note and keep in touch to nurture these new connections. These interviews not only provide valuable information but also help establish relationships that could lead to future opportunities in your desired career path.

Talk with Training Partners

Leveraging your company's training partners and vendors. Build relationships with these external entities by actively engaging in training sessions and company collaborations. Express interest in their industry practices and ask insightful questions to gain deeper knowledge.

Networking with these professionals can provide you with an external perspective on industry trends and potential job opportunities. Additionally, being involved with vendors and training partners can showcase your initiative and eagerness to learn, qualities that are attractive to potential employers.

Don't hesitate to inquire about openings in their companies or seek advice on transitioning into their industry. By leveraging these connections, you can tap into a broader network and gain valuable insights that can significantly support your career transition.

Be Active in the Community

Networking within your community, outside the realms of family, friends, or volunteering, can be a valuable tool. Participate in local business events, such as chamber of commerce meetings, industry-specific seminars, or networking groups. These gatherings are prime opportunities to meet professionals from various fields, providing a broader perspective and potential job leads.

Attend community lectures, workshops, or panel discussions related to your desired industry. Engage in conversations, asking thoughtful questions and sharing insights about your career transition goals. Joining local hobby or interest groups that align with your professional interests can also lead to unexpected connections.

Always maintain a professional demeanor, be transparent about your career aspirations, and listen attentively to others, as this approach can lead to fruitful professional relationships and potential career opportunities.

Talk to Family and Friends

Networking with friends and family for a career transition involves clear communication about your career goals and aspirations. Start by informing them about the type of roles or industries you are interested in transitioning to. Ask if they have contacts in these areas and request introductions or referrals.

Be specific about the kind of help or information you need, whether it's insights into a particular field, company recommendations, or potential job openings. Encourage them to think of you if they come across opportunities that align with your goals. It's also beneficial to engage in conversations about their professional experiences and learnings, as this can provide valuable perspectives and advice.

Remember to express gratitude for their support and keep them updated on your progress, as this nurtures your relationships and keeps them invested in your career journey.

Volunteer in the Community

Volunteering is an effective networking tool, offering opportunities to demonstrate your skills and connect with professionals in your desired field. Choose volunteer roles that align with your career interests or offer transferable skills. While volunteering, take the initiative to engage with other volunteers, organizers, and participants, as they can provide valuable insights and connections.

Showcase your abilities and work ethic, as this can lead to recommendations or job leads from those who witness your contributions first-hand. Actively participate in meetings or planning sessions, offering ideas and showing your ability to work collaboratively. Networking through volunteering isn't just about meeting people; it's also about displaying your skills and dedication in a real-world setting, which can significantly bolster your professional reputation and open doors to new career opportunities.

5

Conclusion

As you've journeyed through "27 Career Transition Tips: Use the Job You Have to Get the Job You Want," you've been equipped with a wealth of strategies to navigate your career pivot successfully. From the chapters on Work Environment, Resume & Interviewing, to Networking, each section has provided you with actionable steps to transform your current position into a stepping stone for your desired career path.

In the Work Environment chapter, you've learned the art of leveraging your present role to build relevant skills and experiences. This includes identifying transferable skills, engaging in projects that align with your future aspirations, and cultivating valuable relationships with mentors and colleagues.

The insights from the Resume & Interviewing chapter have shown you how to tailor your resume to reflect your new career direction and approach interviews with confidence. This section emphasized the importance of articulating your past experiences in a way that resonates with your new industry and framing your career transition as a proactive and positive move.

Lastly, the Networking chapter has opened your eyes to the power of building and nurturing diverse professional relationships. You've discovered how to utilize both informal networks—like those with friends, family, and community members—and formal ones, such as professional associations and platforms like LinkedIn. The significance of informational interviews and the strategic use of volunteering opportunities for networking have also been highlighted.

Now, armed with these insights and tactics, you're better prepared to navigate the complexities of changing careers. This book has aimed not just to guide you but to empower you with the confidence and clarity needed to embark on your new professional journey.

6

Resources

Mind Tools. (n.d.). Changing Career Within Your Organization. Retrieved December 11,2023 from **https://www.mindtools.com/aa8yy78/changing-career-w ithin-your-organization**

Stryker's Career Blog. (April 21). Growing Talent through Employee Resource Groups. Retrieved December 11, 2023 from **https://www.strykercareersblog.com/post/growing-talent- through-employee-resource-groups**

LinkedIn. (n.d.). How Can You Use Job Rotations to Gain Diverse Career Experiences? Retrieved December 11, 2023 from **https://www.linkedin.com/advice/3/how-can-you-use-job- rotations-gain-diverse-career**

Mulawka, Lara. Quill (2019, February 13). How to Network to Transition to a New Career Field. Retrieved on December 11, 2023 from **https://www.quill.com/blog/how-to-network-to- transition-to-a-new-career-field/**

Fielden, Jim. LinkedIn. (2022, September 19). Networking on LinkedIn During a Career Transition. Retrieved on December 11, 2023 from **https://www.linkedin.com/pulse/networking-linkedin-during-career-transition-jim-fielden#:~:text=Joi n%20groups%20related%20to%20your,for%20advice%20and%20networking%20opportunities.**

Indeed. (2023, July 7). Updating Your Resume for a Career Change. Retrieved December 11, 2023, from **https://www.indeed.com/career-advice/resumes-cover-l etters/updating-your-resume-in-a-career-change**

Birt, Jamie. Indeed (2023, November 30). How to use the STAR Interview Response Technique. Retrieved on December 11, 2023 from **https://www.indeed.com/career-advice/interviewing/how -to-use-the-star-interview-response-technique**

Indeed. (2023, March 7). 30-60-90-Day Plan. A Guide with Template and Example. Retrieved December 11, 2023 from **https://www.indeed.com/career-advice/starting-new-job /30-60-90-day-plan**

OpenAI. (2023). ChatGPT (GPT-3.5, GPT-4) [Software]. OpenAI. https://chat.openai.com/